God's Voice for Prayers: 45 Psalms & Prayers

Dee Evans

For information about custom editions, special sales, premium, and bulk purchases, please contact:

authordevans@gmail.com
Rise2Write.com[1]
Rise2Write Publishing LLC

---

1.   https://d.docs.live.net/dc775efeec61d8c3/Desktop/My%20Published%20Books/
God's%20Voice%20Prayers%2045%20psalms%2045/rise2write.com

DEDICATION

THIS PRAYER BOOK IS dedicated to my Husband, Son, Mother, and God-fearing Servants all over the World.

.

INTRODUCTION

1 THESSALONIANS 5:17-18

Pray without ceasing. In everything give thanks: for this is the will of God in Christ Jesus concerning you.

❖

This prayer book consists of 45 prayers from the book of Psalms, with a prayer starter after each Psalm. We often look to man for words and direction when God has provided us with that in the Holy Bible. My goal is to keep God's word at the center and your Holy Spirit on the frontline. The purpose of this book is for it to be your spiritual companion through these difficult times. Each Psalm is a reminder of hope, grace, and God's love for his Children.

These prayers shall bring peace to the soul, spirit, and mind. This prayer book intends to help you redirect your focus on God's word, comfort, and everlasting love.

Please meditate on each prayer daily in a quiet setting with no distractions. I pray that God continues to bless you with understanding, hedge of protection, and spiritual guidance through these times.

May God Bless You and your Families!

PSALMS CHAPTER 4

{4:1} Hear me when I call, O God of my righteousness: thou hast enlarged me [when I was] in distress; have mercy upon me, and hear my prayer. {4:2} O ye sons of men, how long [will ye turn] my glory into shame? [how long] will ye love vanity, [and] seek after leasing? Selah. {4:3} But know that the LORD hath set apart him that is godly for himself: the LORD will hear when I call unto him. {4:4} Stand in awe, and sin not: commune with your own heart upon your bed, and be still. Selah. {4:5} Offer the sacrifices of righteousness, and put your trust in the LORD. {4:6} [There be] many that say, Who will shew us [any] good? LORD, lift thou up the light of thy countenance upon us. {4:7} Thou hast put gladness in my heart, more than in the time [that] their corn and their wine increased. {4:8} I will both lay me down in peace, and sleep: for thou, LORD, only makest me dwell in safety.

❖

Prayer:

Oh Father God in Heaven,

Hear my cry out to you during this time of uncertainty, as I feel Weak and Weary. Strengthen me oh lord. Strengthen my faith. I trust that you are with me in guidance and protection. I will continue to seek your will and put my trust in you with all my heart and soul for deliverance through this challenging time.

In Jesus Name I pray, Amen!

PSALMS CHAPTER 11

{11:1} In the LORD put I my trust: How say ye to my soul, Flee [as] a bird to your mountain? {11:2} For, lo, the wicked bend [their] bow, they make ready their arrow upon the string, that they may privily shoot at the upright in heart. {11:3} If the foundations be destroyed, what can the righteous do? {11:4} The LORD [is] in his holy temple, the LORD'S throne [is] in heaven: his eyes behold, his eyelids try, the children of men. {11:5} The LORD trieth the righteous: but the wicked and him that loveth violence his soul hateth. {11:6} Upon the wicked he shall rain snares, fire and brimstone, and an horrible tempest: [this shall be] the portion of their cup. {11:7} For the righteous LORD loveth righteousness; his countenance doth behold the upright.

❖

Prayer:
Oh Father God in Heaven,

I put my trust in you and you alone oh god! Deliver me from my sins lord, keep me upright in heart and spirit. What I am facing now, I know this too shall pass. I know that you hold shield and protection over the righteous. I ask that you continue to hold shield over your servant for I am daily seeking you.

In Jesus Name I pray, Amen!

PSALMS CHAPTER 16

{16:1} Preserve me, O God: for in thee do I put my trust. {16:2} [O my soul,] thou hast said unto the LORD, Thou [art] my Lord: my goodness [extendeth] not to thee; {16:3} [But] to the saints that [are] in the earth, and [to] the excellent, in whom [is] all my delight. {16:4} Their sorrows shall be multiplied [that] hasten [after] another [god:] their drink offerings of blood will I not offer, nor take up their names into my lips. {16:5} The LORD [is] the portion of mine inheritance and of my cup: thou maintainest my lot. {16:6} The lines are fallen unto me in pleasant [places;] yea, I have a goodly heritage. {16:7} I will bless the LORD, who hath given me counsel: my reins also instruct me in the night seasons. {16:8} I have set the LORD always before me: because [he is] at my right hand, I shall not be moved. {16:9} Therefore my heart is glad, and my glory rejoiceth: my flesh also shall rest in hope. {16:10} For thou wilt not leave my soul in hell; neither wilt thou suffer thine Holy One to see corruption. {16:11} Thou wilt shew me the path of life: in thy presence [is] fulness of joy; at thy right hand [there are] pleasures for evermore.

❖

Prayer:

Oh Father God in Heaven,

I will not be moved by the chaos in front of me. For my ways are focused only on your word and guidance. for my trust is only in you lord. My flesh and soul rest in hope with and I have been delivered from the spirit of fear and anxiety. I ask for your

continuance strength, mercy, and upliftment during these times.
for you i will continue to rest my faith in.

In Jesus Name I pray, Amen!

PSALMS 18:1-6,18:20-23

{18:1} I will love thee, O LORD, my strength. {18:2} The LORD [is] my rock, and my fortress, and my deliverer; my God, my strength, in whom I will trust; my buckler, and the horn of my salvation, [and] my high tower. {18:3} I will call upon the LORD, [who is worthy] to be praised: so shall I be saved from mine enemies. {18:4} The sorrows of death compassed me, and the floods of ungodly men made me afraid. {18:5} The sorrows of hell compassed me about: the snares of death prevented me. {18:6} In my distress I called upon the LORD, and cried unto my God: he heard my voice out of his temple, and my cry came before him, [even] into his ears.

{18:20} The LORD rewarded me according to my righteousness; according to the cleanness of my hands hath he recompensed me. {18:21} For I have kept the ways of the LORD, and have not wickedly departed from my God. {18:22} For all his judgments [were] before me, and I did not put away his statutes from me. {18:23} I was also upright before him, and I kept myself from mine iniquity.

❖

• • • •

PRAYER:

Oh Father God in Heaven,

I ask for strength and deliverance. I will not turn away from your words, laws, or commandments. I ask that you continue to lift me up when I feel weak, shield me from harm, sickness, any unforeseen evil that Is in front of me. I ask for your shield and buckler for protection in front of me and behind me. For I know that you make my way straight and will not guide me into destruction but only save me from it. I am forever thankful for your mercy and grace during the unforeseen.

In Jesus Name I pray, Amen!

PSALMS CHAPTER 19

{19:1} The heavens declare the glory of God; and the firmament sheweth his handywork. {19:2} Day unto day uttereth speech, and night unto night sheweth knowledge. {19:3} [There is] no speech nor language, [where] their voice is not heard. {19:4} Their line is gone out through all the earth, and their words to the end of the world. In them hath he set a tabernacle for the sun, {19:5} Which [is] as a bridegroom coming out of his chamber, [and] rejoiceth as a strong man to run a race. {19:6} His going forth [is] from the end of the heaven, and his circuit unto the ends of it: and there is nothing hid from the heat thereof. {19:7} The law of the LORD [is] perfect, converting the soul: the testimony of the LORD [is] sure, making wise the simple. {19:8} The statutes of the LORD [are] right, rejoicing the heart: the commandment of the LORD [is] pure, enlightening the eyes. {19:9} The fear of the LORD [is] clean, enduring for ever: the judgments of the LORD [are] true [and] righteous altogether. {19:10} More to be desired [are they] than gold, yea, than much fine gold: sweeter also than honey and the honeycomb. {19:11} Moreover by them is thy servant warned: [and] in keeping of them [there is] great reward. {19:12} Who can understand [his] errors? cleanse thou me from secret faults. {19:13} Keep back thy servant also from presumptuous [sins;] let them not have dominion over me: then shall I be upright, and I shall be innocent from the great transgression. {19:14} Let the words of my mouth, and the meditation of my heart, be acceptable in thy sight, O Lord, my strength, and my redeemer.

❖

Prayer:

Oh Father God in Heaven,

Please forgive me for my sins and shortcomings. For your laws and ways are blameless and perfect. I ask for help with enlightening my eyes and spirit to be set only on your word and laws. For I know you hear my voice, my cries, and my heart. Clean me from evil thoughts, clean me from doubt, clean me from fear, clean me from sin, I no longer want to allow sin to have dominion over me. I no longer want to be a slave to fear, doubt, negative thoughts. I seek you for direction. I thank you for your everlasting grace over my foot steps.

In Jesus Name I pray, Amen!

PSALMS CHAPTER 23

{23:1} The LORD [is] my shepherd; I shall not want. {23:2} He maketh me to lie down in green pastures: he leadeth me beside the still waters. {23:3} He restoreth my soul: he leadeth me in the paths of righteousness for his name's sake. {23:4} Yea, though I walk through the valley of the shadow of death, I will fear no evil: for thou [art] with me; thy rod and thy staff they comfort me. {23:5} Thou preparest a table before me in the presence of mine enemies: thou anointest my head with oil; my cup runneth over. {23:6} Surely goodness and mercy shall follow me all the days of my life: and I will dwell in the house of the LORD for ever.

❖

Prayer:

Oh Father God in Heaven,

Thank you for being my comforter during this crisis. Thank you for watching over my soul and not abandoning me. I ask that you continue to lead me and guide me. I ask that you continue to protect me. I know that you are with me and I know that you will not allow my soul to linger into the pits of satan, therefore I will fear no evil. I will only trust in your guidance.

In Jesus Name I pray, Amen!

PSALMS CHAPTER 27

{27:1} The LORD [is] my light and my salvation; whom shall I fear? the LORD [is] the strength of my life; of whom shall I be afraid? {27:2} When the wicked, [even] mine enemies and my foes, came upon me to eat up my flesh, they stumbled and fell. {27:3} Though an host should encamp against me, my heart shall not fear: though war should rise against me, in this [will] I [be] confident. {27:4} One [thing] have I desired of the LORD, that will I seek after; that I may dwell in the house of the LORD all the days of my life, to behold the beauty of the LORD, and to enquire in his temple. {27:5} For in the time of trouble he shall hide me in his pavilion: in the secret of his tabernacle shall he hide me; he shall set me up upon a rock. {27:6} And now shall mine head be lifted up above mine enemies round about me: therefore will I offer in his tabernacle sacrifices of joy; I will sing, yea, I will sing praises unto the LORD. {27:7} Hear, O LORD, [when] I cry with my voice: have mercy also upon me, and answer me. {27:8} [When thou saidst,] Seek ye my face; my heart said unto thee, Thy face, LORD, will I seek. {27:9} Hide not thy face [far] from me; put not thy servant away in anger: thou hast been my help; leave me not, neither forsake me, O God of my salvation. {27:10} When my father and my mother forsake me, then the LORD will take me up. {27:11} Teach me thy way, O LORD, and lead me in a plain path, because of mine enemies. {27:12} Deliver me not over unto the will of mine enemies: for false witnesses are risen up against me, and such as breathe out cruelty. {27:13} [I had fainted,] unless I had believed to see the goodness of the LORD

*in the land of the living. {27:14} Wait on the LORD: be of good
courage, and he shall strengthen thine heart: wait, I say, on the
LORD.*

❖

Prayer:
Oh Father God in Heaven,

*MY BACK is AGAISNT THE WALL lord. I am feeling
weak and weary. I don't know if I can continue on as once before.
I feel my strength weakening. man has forsaken me. The people
the closest to me has turned their backs on me. I will wait on you
lord! I look to you for help, guidance, protection, strength to face
these hard times ahead of me. I ask that you continue to clear my
path, make my vision clearer. I am dying daily through your grace
and leaning on your will and your way lord. I will rejoice in your
unconditional love and I will forever TURN TO YOU.*

In Jesus Name I pray, Amen!

DAY 8

PSALMS 34:1-19

{34:1} I will bless the LORD at all times: his praise [shall] continually [be] in my mouth. {34:2} My soul shall make her boast in the LORD: the humble shall hear [thereof,] and be glad. {34:3} O magnify the LORD with me, and let us exalt his name together. {34:4} I sought the LORD, and he heard me, and delivered me from all my fears. {34:5} They looked unto him, and were lightened: and their faces were not ashamed. {34:6} This poor man cried, and the LORD heard [him,] and saved him out of all his troubles. {34:7} The angel of the LORD encampeth round about them that fear him, and delivereth them. {34:8} O taste and see that the LORD [is] good: blessed [is] the man [that] trusteth in him. {34:9} O fear the LORD, ye his saints: for [there is] no want to them that fear him. {34:10} The young lions do lack, and suffer hunger: but they that seek the LORD shall not want any good [thing.]{34:11} Come, ye children, hearken unto me: I will teach you the fear of the LORD. {34:12} What man [is he that] desireth life, [and] loveth [many] days, that he may see good? {34:13} Keep thy tongue from evil, and thy lips from speaking guile. {34:14} Depart from evil, and do good; seek peace, and pursue it. {34:15} The eyes of the LORD [are] upon the righteous, and his ears [are open] unto their cry. {34:16} The face of the LORD [is] against them that do evil, to cut off the remembrance of them from the earth. {34:17} [The righteous] cry, and the LORD heareth, and delivereth them out of all their troubles. {34:18} The LORD [is] nigh unto them that are of a broken heart; and saveth such as be of a contrite spirit. {34:19}

15

Many [are] the afflictions of the righteous: but the LORD delivereth him out of them all.

❖

Prayer:
Oh Father God in Heaven,

Thank you lord for my daily blessings. Thank you lord for providing, assisting, guiding, directing, leading over my life. Thank you lord for hearing a voice of a sinner. Thank you father. I will forever praise your name, cry aloud and surrender myself to you!

In Jesus Name I pray, Amen!

DAY 9

PSALMS 40:1-11

{40:1} I waited patiently for the LORD; and he inclined unto me, and heard my cry. {40:2} He brought me up also out of an horrible pit, out of the miry clay, and set my feet upon a rock, [and] established my goings. {40:3} And he hath put a new song in my mouth, [even] praise unto our God: many shall see [it,] and fear, and shall trust in the LORD. {40:4} Blessed [is] that man that maketh the LORD his trust, and respecteth not the proud, nor such as turn aside to lies. {40:5} Many, O LORD my God, [are] thy wonderful works [which] thou hast done, and thy thoughts [which are] to us-ward: they cannot be reckoned up in order unto thee: [if] I would declare and speak [of them,] they are more than can be numbered. {40:6} Sacrifice and offering thou didst not desire; mine ears hast thou opened: burnt offering and sin offering hast thou not required. {40:7} Then said I, Lo, I come: in the volume of the book [it is] written of me, {40:8} I delight to do thy will, O my God: yea, thy law [is] within my heart. {40:9} I have preached righteousness in the great congregation: lo, I have not refrained my lips, O LORD, thou knowest. {40:10} I have not hid thy righteousness within my heart; I have declared thy faithfulness and thy salvation: I have not concealed thy lovingkindness and thy truth from the great congregation. {40:11} Withhold not thou thy tender mercies from me, O LORD: let thy lovingkindness and thy truth continually preserve me.

❖

17

Prayer:

Oh Father God in Heaven,

You are my rock, you are my provider, you delivered me from mine enemies. I ask that you continue to protect me from mine enemies. I ask that you Forgive me for my sins. I ask that you continue to strengthen my faith, my obedience, my patience. I pray for wisdom and knowledge. I pray for hedge of protection. I love you lord and i will magnify your name forever and all of eternity lord!

In Jesus Name I pray, Amen!

PSALMS CHAPTER 46

{46:1} God [is] our refuge and strength, a very present help in trouble. {46:2} Therefore will not we fear, though the earth be removed, and though the mountains be carried into the midst of the sea; {46:3} [Though] the waters thereof roar [and] be troubled, [though] the mountains shake with the swelling thereof. Selah. {46:4} [There is] a river, the streams whereof shall make glad the city of God, the holy [place] of the tabernacles of the most High. {46:5} God [is] in the midst of her; she shall not be moved: God shall help her, [and that] right early. {46:6} The heathen raged, the kingdoms were moved: he uttered his voice, the earth melted. {46:7} The LORD of hosts [is] with us; the God of Jacob [is] our refuge. Selah. {46:8} Come, behold the works of the LORD, what desolations he hath made in the earth. {46:9} He maketh wars to cease unto the end of the earth; he breaketh the bow, and cutteth the spear in sunder; he burneth the chariot in the fire. {46:10} Be still, and know that I [am] God: I will be exalted among the heathen, I will be exalted in the earth. {46:11} The LORD of hosts [is] with us; the God of Jacob [is] our refuge. Selah.

❖

Prayer:
Oh Father God in Heaven,
You are my strength during these times of short comings lord. You are my healer, my provider, my strength, my protector, my guidance. Continue to watch over your children lord. For we need

you more than ever in these times. Please stay near me lord and continue to use me. I serve you lord! Thank you lord!

In Jesus Name I pray, Amen!

PSALMS 49:1-15

{49:1} Hear this, all [ye] people; give ear, all [ye] inhabitants of the world: {49:2} Both low and high, rich and poor, together. {49:3} My mouth shall speak of wisdom; and the meditation of my heart [shall be] of understanding. {49:4} I will incline mine ear to a parable: I will open my dark saying upon the harp. {49:5} Wherefore should I fear in the days of evil, [when] the iniquity of my heels shall compass me about? {49:6} They that trust in their wealth, and boast themselves in the multitude of their riches; {49:7} None [of them] can by any means redeem his brother, nor give to God a ransom for him: {49:8} (For the redemption of their soul [is] precious, and it ceaseth for ever:) {49:9} That he should still live for ever, [and] not see corruption. {49:10} For he seeth [that] wise men die, likewise the fool and the brutish person perish, and leave their wealth to others. {49:11} Their inward thought [is, that] their houses [shall continue] for ever, [and] their dwelling places to all generations; they call [their] lands after their own names. {49:12} Nevertheless man [being] in honour abideth not: he is like the beasts [that] perish. {49:13} This their way [is] their folly: yet their posterity approve their sayings. Selah. {49:14} Like sheep they are laid in the grave; death shall feed on them; and the upright shall have dominion over them in the morning; and their beauty shall consume in the grave from their dwelling. {49:15} But God will redeem my soul from the power of the grave: for he shall receive me. Selah.

❖

Prayer:

Oh Father God in Heaven,

Thank you lord for we see that no man on earth is above the power of god. For no riches we store on earth matters in the time of judgement. Only our hearts and soul are weighed. Oh lord please make a clean heart within me. Please show me the areas In my life where i am falling short. Make me over lord. I surrender to being a better reflection of you lord. My purpose is to serve you Lord. My soul quenches for you lord and I will continue to trust in you lord for all the days of my life.

In Jesus Name I pray, Amen!

PSALMS 51:1-15

{51:1} Have mercy upon me, O God, according to thy lovingkindness: according unto the multitude of thy tender mercies blot out my transgressions. {51:2} Wash me throughly from mine iniquity, and cleanse me from my sin. {51:3} For I acknowledge my transgressions: and my sin [is] ever before me. {51:4} Against thee, thee only, have I sinned, and done [this] evil in thy sight: that thou mightest be justified when thou speakest, [and] be clear when thou judgest. {51:5} Behold, I was shapen in iniquity; and in sin did my mother conceive me. {51:6} Behold, thou desirest truth in the inward parts: and in the hidden [part] thou shalt make me to know wisdom. {51:7} Purge me with hyssop, and I shall be clean: wash me, and I shall be whiter than snow. {51:8} Make me to hear joy and gladness; [that] the bones [which] thou hast broken may rejoice. {51:9} Hide thy face from my sins, and blot out all mine iniquities. {51:10} Create in me a clean heart, O God; and renew a right spirit within me. {51:11} Cast me not away from thy presence; and take not thy holy spirit from me. {51:12} Restore unto me the joy of thy salvation; and uphold me [with thy] free spirit. {51:13} [Then] will I teach transgressors thy ways; and sinners shall be converted unto thee. {51:14} Deliver me from bloodguiltiness, O God, thou God of my salvation: [and] my tongue shall sing aloud of thy righteousness. {51:15} O Lord, open thou my lips; and my mouth shall shew forth thy praise.

❖

Prayer:

Oh Father God in Heaven,

I have nothing without you. My life means nothing without you lord. I want to be better. I need you more than ever lord and I ask for your forgiveness as I forgive my trespassers. I ask that you wash away my sins lord. Please make me whole lord through you. renew my mind and spirit that is within me. Have mercy on me lord.

In Jesus Name I pray, Amen!

PSALMS CHAPTER 54

{54:1} Save me, O God, by thy name, and judge me by thy strength. {54:2} Hear my prayer, O God; give ear to the words of my mouth. {54:3} For strangers are risen up against me, and oppressors seek after my soul: they have not set God before them. Selah. {54:4} Behold, God [is] mine helper: the Lord [is] with them that uphold my soul. {54:5} He shall reward evil unto mine enemies: cut them off in thy truth. {54:6} I will freely sacrifice unto thee: I will praise thy name, O LORD; for [it is] good. {54:7} For he hath delivered me out of all trouble: and mine eye hath seen [his desire] upon mine enemies.

❖

Prayer:
Oh Father God in Heaven,
Please hear me lord as I cry unto you. For I am at my lowest, where my vision seems blurry. For I am being attacked lord on all sides. I need you now lord. The enemy is after my soul. I will leave my enemies to you lord to fight on my behalf. Lord, You will never leave me or forsaken me. Make my vision clear again lord! You are my savior, my helper, my redeemer and I need you now to strengthen me. I surrender it all over to you and I will continue to put my faith and trust in you lord!
In Jesus Name I pray, Amen!

PSALMS 55:1-17

{55:1} Give ear to my prayer, O God; and hide not thyself from my supplication. {55:2} Attend unto me, and hear me: I mourn in my complaint, and make a noise; {55:3} Because of the voice of the enemy, because of the oppression of the wicked: for they cast iniquity upon me, and in wrath they hate me. {55:4} My heart is sore pained within me: and the terrors of death are fallen upon me. {55:5} Fearfulness and trembling are come upon me, and horror hath overwhelmed me. {55:6} And I said, Oh that I had wings like a dove! [for then] would I fly away, and be at rest. {55:7} Lo, [then] would I wander far off, [and] remain in the wilderness. Selah. {55:8} I would hasten my escape from the windy storm [and] tempest. {55:9} Destroy, O Lord, [and] divide their tongues: for I have seen violence and strife in the city. {55:10} Day and night they go about it upon the walls thereof: mischief also and sorrow [are] in the midst of it. {55:11} Wickedness [is] in the midst thereof: deceit and guile depart not from her streets. {55:12} For [it was] not an enemy [that] reproached me; then I could have borne [it:] neither [was it] he that hated me [that] did magnify [himself] against me; then I would have hid myself from him: {55:13} But [it was] thou, a man mine equal, my guide, and mine acquaintance. {55:14} We took sweet counsel together, [and] walked unto the house of God in company. {55:15} Let death seize upon them, [and] let them go down quick into hell: for wickedness is in their dwellings, [and] among them. {55:16} As for me, I will call upon God; and the

LORD shall save me. {55:17} Evening, and morning, and at noon, will I pray, and cry aloud: and he shall hear my voice.

❖

Prayer:
Oh Father God in Heaven,

I cast my burden unto you lord. For I know that you are a god of peace, a god of war. You are the god of glory and the god of love! I ask that you deliver me from pain & suffering, deliver me from this storm that I am facing. Deliver me from my enemies, deliver me from evil thoughts. I am ready to see the sunshine and the light at the end of the tunnel lord. Please set me free from my enemies during this battle lord. I trust in you lord and I thank you for never leaving my side.

In Jesus Name I pray, Amen!

PSALMS CHAPTER 57

{57:1} Be merciful unto me, O God, be merciful unto me: for my soul trusteth in thee: yea, in the shadow of thy wings will I make my refuge, until [these] calamities be overpast. {57:2} I will cry unto God most high; unto God that performeth [all things] for me. {57:3} He shall send from heaven, and save [from] the reproach of him that would swallow me up. Selah. God shall send forth his mercy and his truth. {57:4} My soul [is] among lions: [and] I lie [even among] them that are set on fire, [even] the sons of men, whose teeth [are] spears and arrows, and their tongue a sharp sword. {57:5} Be thou exalted, O God, above the heavens; [let] thy glory [be] above all the earth. {57:6} They have prepared a net for my steps; my soul is bowed down: they have digged a pit before me, into the midst whereof they are fallen [themselves.] Selah. {57:7} My heart is fixed, O God, my heart is fixed: I will sing and give praise. {57:8} Awake up, my glory; awake, psaltery and harp: I [myself] will awake early. {57:9} I will praise thee, O Lord, among the people: I will sing unto thee among the nations. {57:10} For thy mercy is great unto the heavens, and thy truth unto the clouds. {57:11} Be thou exalted, O God, above the heavens: [let] thy glory [be] above all the earth.

❖

Prayer:

Oh Father God in Heaven,

I will never stop worshiping you For your mercy and everlasting love and grace over my soul. Thank you for delivering me from the pits and darkness of hell. Thank you lord for restoring my soul, restoring my health, restoring my faith, restoring my finances, restoring my household, restoring my family. I am forever thankful lord for what you are doing over my life. I will never stop serving you lord! Hallelujah!

In Jesus Name I pray, Amen!

PSALMS CHAPTER 60

{60:1} O God, thou hast cast us off, thou hast scattered us, thou hast been displeased; O turn thyself to us again. {60:2} Thou hast made the earth to tremble; thou hast broken it: heal the breaches thereof; for it shaketh. {60:3} Thou hast shewed thy people hard things: thou hast made us to drink the wine of astonishment. {60:4} Thou hast given a banner to them that fear thee, that it may be displayed because of the truth. Selah. {60:5} That thy beloved may be delivered; save [with] thy right hand, and hear me. {60.6} God hath spoken in his holiness; I will rejoice, I will divide Shechem, and mete out the valley of Succoth. {60:7} Gilead [is] mine, and Manasseh [is] mine; Ephraim also [is] the strength of mine head; Judah [is] my lawgiver; {60:8} Moab [is] my washpot; over Edom will I cast out my shoe: Philistia, triumph thou because of me. {60:9} Who will bring me [into] the strong city? who will lead me into Edom? {60:10} [Wilt] not thou, O God, [which] hadst cast us off? and [thou,] O God, [which] didst not go out with our armies? {60:11} Give us help from trouble: for vain [is] the help of man. {60:12} Through God we shall do valiantly: for he [it is that] shall tread down our enemies.

❖

Prayer:
Oh Father God in Heaven,

Please forgive us lord. For we have sinned as a nation and we ask that you continue to touch every soul and deliver this world from the hands of satan. We need you lord to heal the world.

In Jesus Name I pray, Amen!

DAY 17

PSALMS CHAPTER 61

{61:1} Hear my cry, O God; attend unto my prayer. {61:2} *From the end of the earth will I cry unto thee, when my heart is overwhelmed: lead me to the rock [that] is higher than I. {61:3} For thou hast been a shelter for me, [and] a strong tower from the enemy. {61:4} I will abide in thy tabernacle for ever: I will trust in the covert of thy wings. Selah. {61:5} For thou, O God, hast heard my vows: thou hast given [me] the heritage of those that fear thy name. Psalms {61:6} Thou wilt prolong the king's life: [and] his years as many generations. {61:7} He shall abide before God for ever: O prepare mercy and truth, [which] may preserve him. {61:8} So will I sing praise unto thy name for ever, that I may daily perform my vows.*

❖

Prayer:
Oh Father God in Heaven,
Thank you for being my shelter as I face this world. You have proven to me that you will never leave my side. Continue to lead me out of destruction and into my destiny. All my hope and faith is within you lord. I will praise your name and honor your name forever lord.
In Jesus Name I pray, Amen!

DAY 18

PSALMS 62:1-8

{62:1} Truly my soul waiteth upon God: from him [cometh] my salvation. {62:2} He only [is] my rock and my salvation; [he is] my defence; I shall not be greatly moved. {62:3} How long will ye imagine mischief against a man? ye shall be slain all of you: as a bowing wall [shall ye be, and as] a tottering fence. {62:4} They only consult to cast [him] down from his excellency: they delight in lies: they bless with their mouth, but they curse inwardly. Selah. {62:5} My soul, wait thou only upon God; for my expectation [is] from him. {62:6} He only [is] my rock and my salvation: [he is] my defence; I shall not be moved. {62:7} In God [is] my salvation and my glory: the rock of my strength, [and] my refuge, [is] in God. {62:8} Trust in him at all times; [ye] people, pour out your heart before him: God [is] a refuge for us. Selah.

❖

Prayer:
Oh Father God in Heaven,

I trust in your word. I trust in your voice, your direction, your will over my life. My soul yearns for you lord and will not be moved by evil thoughts or energies. You are my rock and salvation. For I know that through you all things are possible. You are in control over my life and I am forever thankful for your mercy and grace.

In Jesus Name I pray, Amen!

DAY 19

PSALMS CHAPTER 63

{63:1} O God, thou [art] my God; early will I seek thee: my soul thirsteth for thee, my flesh longeth for thee in a dry and thirsty land, where no water is; {63:2} To see thy power and thy glory, so [as] I have seen thee in the sanctuary. {63:3} Because thy lovingkindness [is] better than life, my lips shall praise thee. {63:4} Thus will I bless thee while I live: I will lift up my hands in thy name. {63:5} My soul shall be satisfied as [with] marrow and fatness; and my mouth shall praise [thee] with joyful lips: {63:6} When I remember thee upon my bed, [and] meditate on thee in the [night] watches. {63:7} Because thou hast been my help, therefore in the shadow of thy wings will I rejoice. {63:8} My soul followeth hard after thee: thy right hand upholdeth me. {63:9} But those [that] seek my soul, to destroy [it,] shall go into the lower parts of the earth. {63:10} They shall fall by the sword: they shall be a portion for foxes. {63:11} But the king shall rejoice in God; every one that sweareth by him shall glory: but the mouth of them that speak lies shall be stopped.

❖

Prayer:
Oh Father God in Heaven,
I am so thankful for you lord. Thank you for allowing me to be alive and apart of this day. My life is in your hands lord. I shall meditate on your word and laws daily. For I know that joy comes in the morning Lord. Trouble will not last over my life.
In Jesus Name I pray, Amen!

PSALMS CHAPTER 67

{67:1} God be merciful unto us, and bless us; [and] cause his face to shine upon us; Selah. {67:2} That thy way may be known upon earth, thy saving health among all nations. {67:3} Let the people praise thee, O God; let all the people praise thee. {67:4} O let the nations be glad and sing for joy: for thou shalt judge the people righteously, and govern the nations upon earth. Selah. {67:5} Let the people praise thee, O God; let all the people praise thee. {67:6} [Then] shall the earth yield her increase; [and] God, [even] our own God, shall bless us. {67:7} God shall bless us; and all the ends of the earth shall fear him.

❖

Prayer:

Oh Father God in Heaven,

I ask that you be merciful onto us lord. For we have sinned lord and we ask for your forgiveness as a nation. I ask that you heal the sick, the weary, the lost and strengthen the righteous during these times lord. I trust and lean onto your guidance lord and your word.

In Jesus Name I pray, Amen!

PSALMS 69:1-10, 69:32-36

{69:1} Save me, O God; for the waters are come in unto [my]
soul. {69:2} I sink in deep mire, where [there is] no standing: I
am come into deep waters, where the floods overflow me. {69:3}
I am weary of my crying: my throat is dried: mine eyes fail while
I wait for my God. {69:4} They that hate me without a cause
are more than the hairs of mine head: they that would destroy
me, [being] mine enemies wrongfully, are mighty: then I restored
[that] which I took not away. {69:5} O God, thou knowest my
foolishness; and my sins are not hid from thee. {69:6} Let not
them that wait on thee, O Lord GOD of hosts, be ashamed for my
sake: let not those that seek thee be confounded for my sake, O God
of Israel. {69:7} Because for thy sake I have borne reproach; shame
hath covered my face. {69:8} I am become a stranger unto my
brethren, and an alien unto my mother's children. {69:9} For the
zeal of thine house hath eaten me up; and the reproaches of them
that reproached thee are fallen upon me. {69:10} When I wept,
[and chastened] my soul with fasting, that was to my reproach.
{69:32} The humble shall see [this, and] be glad: and your heart
shall live that seek God. {69:33} For the LORD heareth the
poor, and despiseth not his prisoners. {69:34} Let the heaven and
earth praise him, the seas, and every thing that moveth therein.
{69:35} For God will save Zion, and will build the cities of
Judah: that they may dwell there, and have it in possession.
{69:36} The seed also of his servants shall inherit it: and they that
love his name shall dwell therein.

❖

Prayer:

Oh Father God in Heaven,

Save me lord. For I seek after you during this time of weariness. Everyone has turned against me. If I have committed a sin unknowingly against my brethren, please forgive me lord. Lord I know that you see the best in me. You judge my heart and soul. I ask that you deliver me from my persecutors. Deliver me from this low spirit. Uplift my spirit lord. Strengthen my faith.

In Jesus Name I pray, Amen!

PSALMS 71:1-14

{71:1} In thee, O LORD, do I put my trust: let me never be put to confusion. {71:2} Deliver me in thy righteousness, and cause me to escape: incline thine ear unto me, and save me. {71:3} Be thou my strong habitation, whereunto I may continually resort: thou hast given commandment to save me; for thou [art] my rock and my fortress. {71:4} Deliver me, O my God, out of the hand of the wicked, out of the hand of the unrighteous and cruel man. {71:5} For thou [art] my hope, O Lord GOD: [thou art] my trust from my youth. {71:6} By thee have I been holden up from the womb: thou art he that took me out of my mother's bowels: my praise [shall be] continually of thee. {71:7} I am as a wonder unto many; but thou [art] my strong refuge. {71:8} Let my mouth be filled [with] thy praise [and with] thy honour all the day. {71:9} Cast me not off in the time of old age; forsake me not when my strength faileth. {71:10} For mine enemies speak against me; and they that lay wait for my soul take counsel together, {71:11} Saying, God hath forsaken him: persecute and take him; for [there is] none to deliver [him.]{71:12} O God, be not far from me: O my God, make haste for my help. {71:13} Let them be confounded [and] consumed that are adversaries to my soul; let them be covered [with] reproach and dishonour that seek my hurt. {71:14} But I will hope continually, and will yet praise thee more and more.

❖

Prayer:

Oh Father God in Heaven,

Save me lord from the spirit of confusion. Deliver me from the traps of satan. Protect your servant lord. For my enemies are on attack after my soul. I ask that all evil over my life is cast out lord. I ask that you Continue to strengthen my faith, and soul oh lord. I trust in you lord and I am so thankful for your hedge of protection over my life. I am thankful for my soul has been redeemed.

In Jesus Name I pray, Amen!

PSALMS 81:1-8

{81:1} Sing aloud unto God our strength: make a joyful noise unto the God of Jacob. {81:2} Take a psalm, and bring hither the timbrel, the pleasant harp with the psaltery. {81:3} Blow up the trumpet in the new moon, in the time appointed, on our solemn feast day. {81:4} For this [was] a statute for Israel, [and] a law of the God of Jacob. {81:5} This he ordained in Joseph [for] a testimony, when he went out through the land of Egypt: [where] I heard a language [that] I understood not. {81:6} I removed his shoulder from the burden: his hands were delivered from the pots. {81:7} Thou calledst in trouble, and I delivered thee; I answered thee in the secret place of thunder: I proved thee at the waters of Meribah. Selah. {81:8} Hear, O my people, and I will testify unto thee: O Israel, if thou wilt hearken unto me;

❖

Prayer:
Oh Father God in Heaven,
I will never stop worshipping you for your everlasting love over my life and grace. For you have delivered me from the hands of my enemies. You have delivered me from sickness, from heartaches, from hardships. I am so thankful for what you are doing over my life and I receive thy blessings to come. Thank you lord! I continue to pray for strength, wisdom & knowledge, and discernment!
In Jesus Name I pray, Amen!

PSALMS 86:1-13

{86:1} Bow down thine ear, O LORD, hear me: for I [am] poor and needy. {86:2} Preserve my soul; for I [am] holy: O thou my God, save thy servant that trusteth in thee. {86:3} Be merciful unto me, O Lord: for I cry unto thee daily. {86:4} Rejoice the soul of thy servant: for unto thee, O Lord, do I lift up my soul. {86:5} For thou, Lord, [art] good, and ready to forgive; and plenteous in mercy unto all them that call upon thee. {86:6} Give ear, O LORD, unto my prayer; and attend to the voice of my supplications. {86:7} In the day of my trouble I will call upon thee: for thou wilt answer me. {86:8} Among the gods [there is] none like unto thee, O Lord; neither [are there any works] like unto thy works. {86:9} All nations whom thou hast made shall come and worship before thee, O Lord; and shall glorify thy name. {86:10} For thou [art] great, and doest wondrous things: thou [art] God alone. {86:11} Teach me thy way, O LORD; I will walk in thy truth: unite my heart to fear thy name. {86:12} I will praise thee, O Lord my God, with all my heart: and I will glorify thy name for evermore. {86:13} For great [is] thy mercy toward me: and thou hast delivered my soul from the lowest hell.

❖

Prayer:

Oh Father God in Heaven,

I turn to you for help lord. Hear my prayer lord, hear my cry out to you lord. For I need you in these times for guidance, for strength, for mercy. For I am ashamed of where I am and I ask for you to attend to my supplications. For you are a god that is full of love and compassion, longsuffering and plenteous in mercy in truth. I will lean on you for deliverance.

In Jesus Name I pray, amen!

PSALMS 88:1-13

{88:1} O LORD God of my salvation, I have cried day [and] night before thee: {88:2} Let my prayer come before thee: incline thine ear unto my cry; {88:3} For my soul is full of troubles: and my life draweth nigh unto the grave. {88:4} I am counted with them that go down into the pit: I am as a man [that hath] no strength: {88:5} Free among the dead, like the slain that lie in the grave, whom thou rememberest no more: and they are cut off from thy hand. {88:6} Thou hast laid me in the lowest pit, in darkness, in the deeps. {88:7} Thy wrath lieth hard upon me, and thou hast afflicted [me] with all thy waves. Selah. {88:8} Thou hast put away mine acquaintance far from me; thou hast made me an abomination unto them: [I am] shut up, and I cannot come forth. {88:9} Mine eye mourneth by reason of affliction: LORD, I have called daily upon thee, I have stretched out my hands unto thee. {88:10} Wilt thou shew wonders to the dead? shall the dead arise [and] praise thee? Selah. {88:11} Shall thy lovingkindness be declared in the grave? [or] thy faithfulness in destruction? {88:12} Shall thy wonders be known in the dark? and thy righteousness in the land of forgetfulness? {88:13} But unto thee have I cried, O LORD; and in the morning shall my prayer prevent thee.

❖

Prayer:
Oh Father God in Heaven,

Lord please hear my prayer. For I am weak and drowning in my tears. My fears have taken over me and I am tired lord. Please lend an ear and hand to me during my affliction. For I ask for forgiveness. I need you near. Hear my prayer and cast out my fear lord. Restore my soul, restore all areas where I have weakened lord. I pray and cry out to you lord. Please hear me and save me!

In Jesus Name I pray, Amen!

PSALMS CHAPTER 90

{90:1} LORD, thou hast been our dwelling place in all generations. {90:2} Before the mountains were brought forth, or ever thou hadst formed the earth and the world, even from everlasting to everlasting, thou [art] God. {90:3} Thou turnest man to destruction; and sayest, Return, ye children of men. {90:4} For a thousand years in thy sight [are but] as yesterday when it is past, and [as] a watch in the night. {90:5} Thou carriest them away as with a flood; they are [as] a sleep: in the morning [they are] like grass [which] groweth up. {90:6} In the morning it flourisheth, and groweth up; in the evening it is cut down, and withereth. {90:7} For we are consumed by thine anger, and by thy wrath are we troubled. {90:8} Thou hast set our iniquities before thee, our secret [sins] in the light of thy countenance. {90:9} For all our days are passed away in thy wrath: we spend our years as a tale [that is told.]{90:10} The days of our years [are] threescore years and ten; and if by reason of strength [they be] fourscore years, yet [is] their strength labour and sorrow; for it is soon cut off, and we fly away. {90:11} Who knoweth the power of thine anger? even according to thy fear, [so is] thy wrath. {90:12} So teach [us] to number our days, that we may apply [our] hearts unto wisdom. {90:13} Return, O LORD, how long? and let it repent thee concerning thy servants. {90:14} O satisfy us early with thy mercy; that we may rejoice and be glad all our days. {90:15} Make us glad according to the days [wherein] thou hast afflicted us, [and] the years [wherein] we have seen evil. {90:16} Let thy work appear unto thy servants, and thy glory unto their *children. {90:17} And let the beauty of the LORD our God be upon us: and establish thou the work of our hands upon us; yea, the work of our hands establish thou it.*

❖

Prayer:

Oh Father God in Heaven,

I am so thankful that you are here, present in my life during my trials and tribulations. for allowing me to overcome my afflictions lord. Thank you lord for being my dwelling place. Thanks for being my deliverer! Please continue to strengthen me, strengthen my wisdom and knowledge, my discernment, my judgments. Guide my path lord. I sing praises and honor your name forever! Hallelujah!

In Jesus Name I pray, Amen!

PSALMS CHAPTER 91

{91:1} He that dwelleth in the secret place of the most High shall abide under the shadow of the Almighty. {91:2} I will say of the LORD, [He is] my refuge and my fortress: my God; in him will I trust. {91:3} Surely he shall deliver thee from the snare of the fowler, [and] from the noisome pestilence. {91:4} He shall cover thee with his feathers, and under his wings shalt thou trust: his truth [shall be thy] shield and buckler. {91:5} Thou shalt not be afraid for the terror by night; [nor] for the arrow [that] flieth by day; {91:6} [Nor] for the pestilence [that] walketh in darkness; [nor] for the destruction [that] wasteth at noonday. {91:7} A thousand shall fall at thy side, and ten thousand at thy right hand; [but] it shall not come nigh thee. {91:8} Only with thine eyes shalt thou behold and see the reward of the wicked. {91:9} Because thou hast made the LORD, [which is] my refuge, [even] the most High, thy habitation; {91:10} There shall no evil befall thee, neither shall any plague come nigh thy dwelling. {91:11} For he shall give his angels charge over thee, to keep thee in all thy ways. {91:12} They shall bear thee up in [their] hands, lest thou dash thy foot against a stone. {91:13} Thou shalt tread upon the lion and adder: the young lion and the dragon shalt thou trample under feet. {91:14} Because he hath set his love upon me, therefore will I deliver him: I will set him on high, because he hath known my name. {91:15} He shall call upon me, and I will answer him: I [will be] with him in trouble; I will deliver him, and honour him. {91:16} With long life will I satisfy him, and shew him my salvation.

❖

Prayer:

Oh Father God in Heaven,

No evil formed against me shall prosper. You have known me from the womb and ordered your hedge of protection over my life. Therefore, I will not be defeated against the enemy lord. I am covered in the blood of jesus. You have delivered me from satan's scheme against my life lord. You are faithful and true, you are my protector, you are my refuge and my fortress, my trust, my faith resides in you lord! You are faithful to the righteous! I seek you daily lord! Thank you for your grace lord and unconditional love!

In Jesus Name I pray, Amen!

PSALMS CHAPTER 93

{93:1} The LORD reigneth, he is clothed with majesty; the LORD is clothed with strength, [wherewith] he hath girded himself: the world also is stablished, that it cannot be moved. {93:2} Thy throne [is] established of old: thou [art] from everlasting. {93:3} The floods have lifted up, O LORD, the floods have lifted up their voice; the floods lift up their waves. {93:4} The LORD on high [is] mightier than the noise of many waters, [yea, than] the mighty waves of the sea. {93:5} Thy testimonies are very sure: holiness becometh thine house, O LORD, for ever.

❖

Prayer:

Oh Father God in Heaven,

No battle is to big for you lord. You sit high and watch over your children. You are undefeated lord! I give myself to you daily lord. I trust in your will over my life. Thank you for my daily blessings lord!

In Jesus Name I pray, Amen!

PSALMS CHAPTER 95

{95:1} O come, let us sing unto the LORD: let us make a joyful noise to the rock of our salvation. {95:2} Let us come before his presence with thanksgiving, and make a joyful noise unto him with psalms. {95:3} For the LORD [is] a great God, and a great King above all gods. {95:4} In his hand [are] the deep places of the earth: the strength of the hills [is] his also. {95:5} The sea [is] his, and he made it: and his hands formed the dry [land.]{95:6} O come, let us worship and bow down: let us kneel before the LORD our maker. {95:7} For he [is] our God; and we [are] the people of his pasture, and the sheep of his hand. To day if ye will hear his voice, {95:8} Harden not your heart, as in the provocation, [and as in] the day of temptation in the wilderness: {95:9} When your fathers tempted me, proved me, and saw my work. {95:10} Forty years long was I grieved with [this] generation, and said, It [is] a people that do err in their heart, and they have not known my ways: {95:11} Unto whom I sware in my wrath that they should not enter into my rest.

❖

• • • •

PRAYER:

Oh Father God in Heaven,

I stand before you as your humble servant. I ask that you forgive me for my sins. I ask that you continue to guide me, shield me and deliver me from any temptations set before me. I am here to bow down to you lord and I am here to worship you. I hear your voice lord. I belong to you lord. I kneel before you with my heart and soul. I ask for strength, endurance, and grace.

Thank you lord for never abandoning me!

In Jesus Name I pray, Amen!

PSALMS CHAPTER 100

{100:1} Make a joyful noise unto the LORD, all ye lands. {100:2} Serve the LORD with gladness: come before his presence with singing. {100:3} Know ye that the LORD he [is] God: [it is] he [that] hath made us, and not we ourselves; [we are] his people, and the sheep of his pasture. {100:4} Enter into his gates with thanksgiving, [and] into his courts with praise: be thankful unto him, [and] bless his name. {100:5} For the LORD [is] good; his mercy [is] everlasting; and his truth [endureth] to all generations.

❖

Prayer:

Oh Father God in Heaven,

How can I not serve you with gladness in my heart. I am so thankful for your grace. I am so thankful for my daily blessings. I have no idea where I would be without you lord. I know my life serves a purpose and sometimes I derail from that purpose. I ask that you continue to guide my steps lord into my purpose. I am so thankful for what you are doing over my life. I will forever bless your name lord.

In Jesus Name I pray, Amen!

PSALMS 103:1-14

{103:1} Bless the LORD, O my soul: and all that is within me, [bless] his holy name. {103:2} Bless the LORD, O my soul, and forget not all his benefits: {103:3} Who forgiveth all thine iniquities; who healeth all thy diseases; {103:4} Who redeemeth thy life from destruction; who crowneth thee with lovingkindness and tender mercies; {103:5} Who satisfieth thy mouth with good [things; so that] thy youth is renewed like the eagle's. {103:6} The LORD executeth righteousness and judgment for all that are oppressed. {103:7} He made known his ways unto Moses, his acts unto the children of Israel. {103:8} The LORD [is] merciful and gracious, slow to anger, and plenteous in mercy. {103:9} He will not always chide: neither will he keep [his anger] for ever. {103:10} He hath not dealt with us after our sins; nor rewarded us according to our iniquities. {103:11} For as the heaven is high above the earth, [so] great is his mercy toward them that fear him. {103:12} As far as the east is from the west, [so] far hath he removed our transgressions from us. {103:13} Like as a father pitieth [his] children, [so] the LORD pitieth them that fear him. {103:14} For he knoweth our frame; he remembereth that we [are] dust.

❖

Prayer:
Oh Father God in Heaven,
Thank you for your everlasting mercy over my life during these times that I fall short. During the times that I stray away

from your word, keeping your commandments and laws. I am dying daily Lord, Please forgive me for my sins. Continue to strengthen me lord. I give you glory lord, for you are slow to anger and plenteous in mercy. I ask for mercy and grace over my soul lord. I surrender to you lord!

In Jesus Name I pray, Amen!

PSALMS 109:1-14

{109:1} Hold not thy peace, O God of my praise; {109:2} For the mouth of the wicked and the mouth of the deceitful are opened against me: they have spoken against me with a lying tongue. {109:3} They compassed me about also with words of hatred; and fought against me without a cause. {109:4} For my love they are my adversaries: but I [give myself unto] prayer. {109:5} And they have rewarded me evil for good, and hatred for my love. {109:6} Set thou a wicked man over him: and let Satan stand at his right hand. {109:7} When he shall be judged, let him be condemned: and let his prayer become sin. {109:8} Let his days be few; [and] let another take his office. {109:9} Let his children be fatherless, and his wife a widow. {109:10} Let his children be continually vagabonds, and beg: let them seek [their bread] also out of their desolate places. {109:11} Let the extortioner catch all that he hath; and let the strangers spoil his labour. {109:12} Let there be none to extend mercy unto him: neither let there be any to favour his fatherless children. {109:13} Let his posterity be cut off; [and] in the generation following let their name be blotted out. {109:14} Let the iniquity of his fathers be remembered with the LORD; and let not the sin of his mother be blotted out.

❖

Prayer:
Oh Father God in Heaven,
Save my soul lord, deliver my soul for the enemy is on attack over my life. It will not work, satan will not win! For I am a

child of god, I am your child lord! The wicked cannot and shall not touch me. I know you are with me oh lord. I know my soul is protected lord and I am saved according to my righteousness. I ask that you continue to protect me and save me from the wicked. I find grace, truth, peace, favor, joy, honor, in your name lord! Hallelujah!

In Jesus Name I pray, Amen!

PSALMS CHAPTER 111

{111:1} Praise ye the LORD. I will praise the LORD with [my] whole heart, in the assembly of the upright, and [in] the congregation. {111:2} The works of the LORD [are] great, sought out of all them that have pleasure therein. {111:3} His work [is] honourable and glorious: and his righteousness endureth for ever. {111:4} He hath made his wonderful works to be remembered: the LORD [is] gracious and full of compassion. {111:5} He hath given meat unto them that fear him: he will ever be mindful of his covenant. {111:6} He hath shewed his people the power of his works, that he may give them the heritage of the heathen. {111:7} The works of his hands [are] verity and judgment; all his commandments [are] sure. {111:8} They stand fast for ever and ever, [and are] done in truth and uprightness. {111:9} He sent redemption unto his people: he hath commanded his covenant for ever: holy and reverend [is] his name. {111:10} The fear of the LORD [is] the beginning of wisdom: a good understanding have all they that do [his commandments:] his praise endureth for ever.

❖

Prayer:

Oh Father God in Heaven,

I wont stop praising your name lord. For you are honorable and glorious. You deserve to be praised for your works are great. I am never going backwards lord. I am only moving forward, focused on your word, laws, and commandments lord. For I only fear you lord. You have the victory over my life lord! I will never stop worshiping you! Hallelujah!

In Jesus Name I pray, Amen!

PSALMS CHAPTER 116

{116:1} I love the LORD, because he hath heard my voice [and] my supplications. {116:2} Because he hath inclined his ear unto me, therefore will I call upon [him] as long as I live. {116:3} The sorrows of death compassed me, and the pains of hell gat hold upon me: I found trouble and sorrow. {116:4} Then called I upon the name of the LORD; O LORD, I beseech thee, deliver my soul. {116:5} Gracious [is] the LORD, and righteous; yea, our God [is] merciful. {116:6} The LORD preserveth the simple: I was brought low, and he helped me. {116:7} Return unto thy rest, O my soul; for the LORD hath dealt bountifully with thee. {116:8} For thou hast delivered my soul from death, mine eyes from tears, [and] my feet from falling. {116:9} I will walk before the LORD in the land of the living. {116:10} I believed, therefore have I spoken: I was greatly afflicted: {116:11} I said in my haste, All men [are] liars. {116:12} What shall I render unto the LORD [for] all his benefits toward me? {116:13} I will take the cup of salvation, and call upon the name of the LORD. {116:14} I will pay my vows unto the LORD now in the presence of all his people. {116:15} Precious in the sight of the LORD [is] the death of his saints. {116:16} O LORD, truly I [am] thy servant; I [am] thy servant, [and] the son of thine handmaid: thou hast loosed my bonds. {116:17} I will offer to thee the sacrifice of thanksgiving, and will call upon the name of the LORD. {116:18} I will pay my vows unto the LORD now in the presence of all his people, {116:19} In the courts of the LORD'S house, in the midst of thee, O Jerusalem. Praise ye the LORD.

❖

Prayer:
Oh Father God in Heaven,

Thank you for hearing my prayer lord. Thank you for never leaving my side. Thank you for being right here with me during my troubles lord. During the good and guiding me through the bad. For you never place more on me than I can bear. I am so blessed lord, for my affliction has made me stronger lord. Please continue to guide me, direct my paths, and strengthen my wisdom and knowledge. I trust your will and way. I will forever call on your name lord!

In Jesus Name I pray, Amen!

DAY 35

PSALMS CHAPTER 117

{117:1} O praise the LORD, all ye nations: praise him, all ye people. {117:2} For his merciful kindness is great toward us: and the truth of the LORD [endureth] for ever. Praise ye the LORD.

❖

Prayer:
Oh Father God in Heaven,

Seated in majesty, I praise your name forever lord. You have made the impossible, possible over my life lord! I will never look back and serve the wicked. For I shall only serve you lord for the rest of my days! My cup is overflown with thy blessings. I will praise you forever!

In Jesus Name I pray, Amen!

DAY 36

PSALMS CHAPTER 121

{121:1} I will lift up mine eyes unto the hills, from whence cometh my help. {121:2} My help [cometh] from the LORD, which made heaven and earth. {121:3} He will not suffer thy foot to be moved: he that keepeth thee will not slumber. {121:4} Behold, he that keepeth Israel shall neither slumber nor sleep. {121:5} The LORD [is] thy keeper: the LORD [is] thy shade upon thy right hand. {121:6} The sun shall not smite thee by day, nor the moon by night. {121:7} The LORD shall preserve thee from all evil: he shall preserve thy soul. {121:8} The LORD shall preserve thy going out and thy coming in from this time forth, and even for evermore.

❖

Prayer:
Oh Father God in Heaven,
My help comes from you lord. I trust in you and not man to deliver me lord. I will not be moved by what I am facing. I know you will make a way for your servant. You shall preserve my soul lord. I trust in you for deliverance. I praise you for rescuing me and I am grateful for you saving me lord!
In Jesus Name I pray, Amen!

PSALMS CHAPTER 128

{128:1} Blessed [is] every one that feareth the LORD; that walketh in his ways. {128:2} For thou shalt eat the labour of thine hands: happy [shalt] thou [be,] and [it shall be] well with thee. {128:3} Thy wife [shall be] as a fruitful vine by the sides of thine house: thy children like olive plants round about thy table. {128:4} Behold, that thus shall the man be blessed that feareth the LORD. {128:5} The LORD shall bless thee out of Zion: and thou shalt see the good of Jerusalem all the days of thy life. {128:6} Yea, thou shalt see thy children's children, [and] peace upon Israel.

❖

Prayer:

Oh Father God in Heaven,

Thank you for the blessing of family and the blessing of children. I pray to see and watch generations raise up and serve you lord. I ask for guidance to be a blessing to others and serve others through your word lord. I ask for wisdom and knowledge. Please continue to strengthen me lord. For I am forever thankful for your everlasting love, grace, and mercy!

In Jesus Name I pray, Amen!

PSALMS CHAPTER 130

{130:1} Out of the depths have I cried unto thee, O LORD. {130:2} Lord, hear my voice: let thine ears be attentive to the voice of my supplications. {130:3} If thou, LORD, shouldest mark iniquities, O Lord, who shall stand? {130:4} But [there is] forgiveness with thee, that thou mayest be feared. {130:5} I wait for the LORD, my soul doth wait, and in his word do I hope. {130:6} My soul [waiteth] for the Lord more than they that watch for the morning: [I say, more than] they that watch for the morning. {130:7} Let Israel hope in the LORD: for with the LORD [there is] mercy, and with him [is] plenteous redemption. {130:8} And he shall redeem Israel from all his iniquities.

❖

Prayer:
Oh Father God in Heaven,

I need you right now, more than ever lord. For my heart is heavy. I am weary and enduring more than I can bare lord. I refuse to give up. I need you Lord, Please save my soul. I will continue to trust in you and stand still in faith. I will continue to wait on your deliverance lord. I will continue to surrender my life over to you lord. I ask for healing and redemption lord.

In Jesus Name I pray, Amen!

PSALMS 139:1-17

{139:1} O LORD, thou hast searched me, and known [me.]{139:2} Thou knowest my downsitting and mine uprising, thou understandest my thought afar off. {139:3} Thou compassest my path and my lying down, and art acquainted [with] all my ways. {139:4} For [there is] not a word in my tongue, [but,] lo, O LORD, thou knowest it altogether. {139:5} Thou hast beset me behind and before, and laid thine hand upon me. {139:6} [Such] knowledge [is] too wonderful for me; it is high, I cannot [attain] unto it. {139:7} Whither shall I go from thy spirit? or whither shall I flee from thy presence? {139:8} If I ascend up into heaven, thou [art] there: if I make my bed in hell, behold, thou [art there.]{139:9} [If] I take the wings of the morning, [and] dwell in the uttermost parts of the sea; {139:10} Even there shall thy hand lead me, and thy right hand shall hold me. {139:11} If I say, Surely the darkness shall cover me; even the night shall be light about me. {139:12} Yea, the darkness hideth not from thee; but the night shineth as the day: the darkness and the light [are] both alike [to thee.]{139:13} For thou hast possessed my reins: thou hast covered me in my mother's womb. {139:14} I will praise thee; for I am fearfully [and] wonderfully made: marvellous [are] thy works; and [that] my soul knoweth right well. {139:15} My substance was not hid from thee, when I was made in secret, [and] curiously wrought in the lowest parts of the earth. {139:16} Thine eyes did see my substance, yet being unperfect; and in thy book all [my members] were written, [which] in continuance were fashioned, when [as yet there was] none of them. {139:17} How *precious also are thy thoughts unto me, O God! how great is the sum of them!*

❖

Prayer:
Oh Father God in Heaven,

Alpha and omega! The victory belongs to you lord, for you have wonderfully made me and covered me in my mother's womb. You know my heart and thoughts. I am thankful for your protection and guidance. How great you are oh lord. How worthy you are to be praised. I love you forever lord!

In Jesus Name I pray, Amen!

DAY 40

PSALMS CHAPTER 141

{141:1} LORD, I cry unto thee: make haste unto me; give ear unto my voice, when I cry unto thee. {141:2} Let my prayer be set forth before thee [as] incense; [and] the lifting up of my hands [as] the evening sacrifice. {141:3} Set a watch, O LORD, before my mouth; keep the door of my lips. {141:4} Incline not my heart to [any] evil thing, to practise wicked works with men that work iniquity: and let me not eat of their dainties. {141:5} Let the righteous smite me; [it shall be] a kindness: and let him reprove me; [it shall be] an excellent oil, [which] shall not break my head: for yet my prayer also [shall be] in their calamities. {141:6} When their judges are overthrown in stony places, they shall hear my words; for they are sweet. {141:7} Our bones are scattered at the grave's mouth, as when one cutteth and cleaveth [wood] upon the earth. {141:8} But mine eyes [are] unto thee, O GOD the Lord: in thee is my trust; leave not my soul destitute. {141:9} Keep me from the snares [which] they have laid for me, and the gins of the workers of iniquity. {141:10} Let the wicked fall into their own nets, whilst that I withal escape.

❖

Prayer:
Oh Father God in Heaven,
I lift my hands to you lord. I cry onto you lord. For I know you shall hear my words. Please keep tame of my mouth, and lips lord. Deliver me from my sins lord. Please make me over and renew my mind and thoughts. Please do not leave my soul in destitute.

79

Protect me from evil and mine enemies. Deliver me from going down the wrong path. Stop me in my tracks lord. Deliver me from all that doesn't mean me any good. Continue to surround me around your angels lord and ones that are for me lord. Hear this prayer of your servant!

In Jesus Name I pray, Amen!

DAY 41

PSALMS CHAPTER 142

{142:1} I cried unto the LORD with my voice; with my voice unto the LORD did I make my supplication. {142:2} I poured out my complaint before him; I shewed before him my trouble. {142:3} When my spirit was overwhelmed within me, then thou knewest my path. In the way wherein I walked have they privily laid a snare for me. {142:4} I looked on [my] right hand, and beheld, but [there was] no man that would know me: refuge failed me; no man cared for my soul. {142:5} I cried unto thee, O LORD: I said, Thou [art] my refuge [and] my portion in the land of the living. {142:6} Attend unto my cry; for I am brought very low: deliver me from my persecutors; for they are stronger than I. {142:7} Bring my soul out of prison, that I may praise thy name: the righteous shall compass me about; for thou shalt deal bountifully with me.

❖

Prayer:
Oh Father God in Heaven,
Deliver me from my enemies and my persecutors. For my strength is weakening and I need you lord to uphold my soul. Favor me against the wicked. Favor me lord. My soul cried to you lord. I will submit to your will lord! I will praise your name!
In Jesus Name I pray, Amen!

PSALMS 147:1-12

{147:1} Praise ye the LORD: for [it is] good to sing praises unto our God; for [it is] pleasant; [and] praise is comely. {147:2} The LORD doth build up Jerusalem: he gathereth together the outcasts of Israel. {147:3} He healeth the broken in heart, and bindeth up their wounds. {147:4} He telleth the number of the stars; he calleth them all by [their] names. {147:5} Great [is] our Lord, and of great power: his understanding [is] infinite. {147:6} The LORD lifteth up the meek: he casteth the wicked down to the ground. {147:7} Sing unto the LORD with thanksgiving; sing praise upon the harp unto our God: {147:8} Who covereth the heaven with clouds, who prepareth rain for the earth, who maketh grass to grow upon the mountains. {147:9} He giveth to the beast his food, [and] to the young ravens which cry. {147:10} He delighteth not in the strength of the horse: he taketh not pleasure in the legs of a man. {147:11} The LORD taketh pleasure in them that fear him, in those that hope in his mercy. {147:12} Praise the LORD, O Jerusalem; praise thy God, O Zion.

❖

Prayer:
Oh Father God in Heaven,
Thank you lord for all that you have done over my life. Thank you for your favor on my soul. I am so thankful for my daily blessings. Great is your power and dominion over the earth. I am so thankful for your infinite understanding and love.

In Jesus Name I pray, Amen!

DAY 43

PSALMS CHAPTER 148

{148:1} Praise ye the LORD. Praise ye the LORD from the heavens: praise him in the heights. {148:2} Praise ye him, all his angels: praise ye him, all his hosts. {148:3} Praise ye him, sun and moon: praise him, all ye stars of light. {148:4} Praise him, ye heavens of heavens, and ye waters that [be] above the heavens. {148:5} Let them praise the name of the LORD: for he commanded, and they were created. {148:6} He hath also stablished them for ever and ever: he hath made a decree which shall not pass. {148:7} Praise the LORD from the earth, ye dragons, and all deeps: {148:8} Fire, and hail; snow, and vapours; stormy wind fulfilling his word: {148:9} Mountains, and all hills; fruitful trees, and all cedars: {148:10} Beasts, and all cattle; creeping things, and flying fowl: {148:11} Kings of the earth, and all people; princes, and all judges of the earth: {148:12} Both young men, and maidens; old men, and children: {148:13} Let them praise the name of the LORD: for his name alone is excellent; his glory [is] above the earth and heaven. {148:14} He also exalteth the horn of his people, the praise of all his saints; [even] of the children of Israel, a people near unto him. Praise ye the LORD.

❖

Prayer:
Oh Father God in Heaven,
Thank you lord! I am so thankful for your creations of this earth. how patient you were with creation. My life is in your

hands lord. You are worthy to be praised from generations to eternity. Death will not separate me from you lord. All the glory belongs to you lord! I will forever worship and praise your name lord.

In Jesus Name I pray, Amen!

PSALMS CHAPTER 149

{149:1} Praise ye the LORD. Sing unto the LORD a new song, [and] his praise in the congregation of saints. {149:2} Let Israel rejoice in him that made him: let the children of Zion be joyful in their King. {149:3} Let them praise his name in the dance: let them sing praises unto him with the timbrel and harp. {149:4} For the LORD taketh pleasure in his people: he will beautify the meek with salvation. {149:5} Let the saints be joyful in glory: let them sing aloud upon their beds. {149:6} [Let] the high [praises] of God [be] in their mouth, and a twoedged sword in their hand; {149:7} To execute vengeance upon the heathen, [and] punishments upon the people; {149:8} To bind their kings with chains, and their nobles with fetters of iron; {149:9} To execute upon them the judgment written: this honour have all his saints. Praise ye the LORD.

❖

Prayer:
Oh Father God in Heaven,
Thank you for this day lord. I am so thankful for your daily blessings. You have saved me from my enemies, you have saved me from the unforeseen. For you protect the righteous and guide your children! I praise and bless your name lord. I love you forever lord. You are mighty and honorable. The alpha and the omega! Thank you lord!
In Jesus Name I pray, Amen!

PSALMS CHAPTER 150

{150:1} Praise ye the LORD. Praise God in his sanctuary: praise him in the firmament of his power. {150:2} Praise him for his mighty acts: praise him according to his excellent greatness. {150:3} Praise him with the sound of the trumpet: praise him with the psaltery and harp. {150:4} Praise him with the timbrel and dance: praise him with stringed instruments and organs. {150:5} Praise him upon the loud cymbals: praise him upon the high sounding cymbals. {150:6} Let everything that hath breath praise the LORD. Praise ye the LORD.

❖

Prayer:

Oh Father God in Heaven,

How can I not praise your name. for I will always bless your name. every praise is to you lord. You have strengthen me, delivered me, blessed me, protected me, healed me, guided me! And you continue to commit such acts over my life daily! I believe in you lord because the battles I face is not mine. Every battle is yours lord. For you shall fight for me and I shall hold my peace and continue to stand firm in faith. Serving you and only you! Hallelujah!

In Jesus Name I pray, Amen!

Keys to Growing Spiritually daily:

✓ **Reading your Bible daily**
✓ **Praying 3x daily**

✓ **Fasting once a month (24hr fast No food)**
✓ **Chapter Meditation (4 times a week)**
✓ **Keeping the Commandments of the Most High God**
✓ **Dying daily through Repentance & Surrendering to God**

I Pray that this prayer book has been a blessing for you!

The purpose of this book was to create a daily routine of prayer and meditation on God's word. I pray you continue to seek the Most High God daily.

Thanks for Reading and don't forget to Share!

Here are more ways to Stay Connected:

Website: https://linktr.ee/authordevans

Please like me on Facebook:

@Authordeeevans

www.facebook.com/authordeeevans/[1]

Follow me on Instagram:

@Authordevans

www.instagram.com/authordevans/[2]

Subscribe to my YouTube channel:

www.youtube.com/c/LifeCoachDee7[3]

Follow my Poetry & Inspiration Podcast:

Spotify:

https://open.spotify.com/show/
3c118ZiFg2x6CxBbW05Es6...[4]

Apple Podcast:

https://podcasts.apple.com/.../dee-poetry.../id1662221385[5]

---

1.   http://www.facebook.com/authordeeevans/

2.   http://www.instagram.com/authordevans/

3.   http://www.youtube.com/c/LifeCoachDee7

4.   https://open.spotify.com/show/
      3c118ZiFg2x6CxBbW05Es6?si=HXpC030vSJaDYh3xcLXzYg&fbclid=IwAR28
      3XCtgLXgkjsLydOEKelOwrZql3bkVHb4QntaZ4Bm99uQoxbuMW-Oz0g

5.   https://podcasts.apple.com/us/podcast/dee-poetry-inspiration-podcast/
      id1662221385?fbclid=IwAR37eRBRf2qMVveRRKl9REgXlw9VIjiltdobkLYyn
      XscASVWjgFkih4w9Zw

MORE BOOKS & JOURNALS FROM DEE

• • • •

"DEVOTION, INSPIRATION & God's Word"

"Rise up in Faith: Forgiveness & Repentance"

"30-Day Devotional & Inspiration for the Single Mom"

"Thoughts from a Black Woman"

"Lust, Pain & Love: A Poetry Collection"

"90-Day Gratitude Journal 4 Men"

"Her Price is far above Rubies: 90-day Self-Reflection Journal"

ABOUT THE AUTHOR

Dee Evans is a servant of the Most High, a Wife, and Mother. She prides herself on being a diverse inspirational writer.
Dee is the Founder and CEO of Rise2Write Publishing LLC, 2x Podcast Host, Blogger, Course developer, and Certified Professional Life Coach.
If interested in talking with Dee please visit:
www.rise2write.com

www.ingramcontent.com/pod-product-compliance
Lightning Source LLC
Chambersburg PA
CBHW060439090426
42733CB00011B/2335